MW00950885

CHINESE TAKEOUT

Welcome to the tantalizing world of the Air-Fried Chinese Takeaway! As the author of this delectable recipe book, I am thrilled to share with you a collection of mouthwatering Chinese dishes, all prepared effortlessly using the wonders of an air fryer. In these pages, you will discover 50 easy-to-follow recipes that encompass the rich and diverse flavors of Chinese cuisine, fused harmoniously with the magic of air frying.

Just like the gentle breeze that caresses our culinary creations, the air fryer breathes new life into traditional Chinese favorites, elevating them to an unparalleled level of crispiness and tenderness. Prepare to embark on a tantalizing journey, where fragrant spices, succulent meats, and vibrant vegetables intertwine in a symphony of taste and texture. Whether you're a seasoned chef or a curious novice, these recipes offer a delightful fusion of convenience and authenticity, granting you the freedom to savor the true essence of Chinese cooking within the comfort of your own kitchen.

Join me as we celebrate the art of modern Chinese cuisine, reimagined with the brilliance of air frying technology. From crispy dumplings and sticky-sweet ribs to tangy orange-glazed chicken and delicate sesame tofu, my recipe book will undoubtedly become your go-to guide for flavorful, wholesome, and fuss-free dishes. So, let the irresistible aromas beckon you, and may each recipe kindle the joy of creating unforgettable feasts for your loved ones. Happy air frying!

Julia

1. AIR FRIED DUMPLINGS

A delightful way to begin our air-fried Chinese culinary journey is with these delectable Air Fried Dumplings. These bite-sized parcels of savory goodness are perfectly crisp on the outside, while retaining their juicy fillings within. Paired with a tangy dipping sauce, they make for an irresistible appetizer or a delightful addition to any meal. So let's gather our ingredients and embark on this flavor-packed adventure!

Ingredients

- 12 dumplings of your choice (pork, chicken, vegetable, etc.)
- 1 tablespoon vegetable oil
- Dipping sauce of your preference (soy sauce, vinegar, chili oil, etc.)

1. Preheat your air fryer to 375°F (190°C). Allow it to reach the desired temperature for a few minutes while we prepare the dumplings.
2. Brush the air fryer basket or tray with a thin coating of vegetable oil to prevent sticking.
3. Place the dumplings in a single layer in the air fryer basket or tray, leaving a little space between each dumpling.
4. Slide the basket or tray into the preheated air fryer and cook the dumplings for 10 minutes. Midway through cooking, open the air fryer and give the basket or tray a gentle shake to ensure even browning.
5. Once the cooking time is complete, carefully remove the air-fried dumplings from the air fryer using tongs or a spatula. Be cautious as they will be hot!
6. Serve the air-fried dumplings immediately with your preferred dipping sauce. The combination of the crisp, golden exterior and the succulent filling will tantalize your taste buds.

Indulge in the delightfully crispy exterior and juicy flavors of these Air Fried Dumplings. They make for a charming appetizer or a delightful main course when accompanied by a vibrant side dish. Enjoy the authentic taste of Chinese cuisine with the convenience of your air fryer. Happy cooking!

2. SPRING ROLLS

A delectable Chinese classic, these Crispy Air Fried Spring Rolls will transport your taste buds to the bustling streets of Asia. Imagine biting into a delicate, golden-brown shell, only to reveal a tantalizing filling of fresh vegetables and aromatic seasonings. This recipe yields enough for a delightful meal for two, perfect for sharing or savoring all by yourself.

Ingredients

- 8 spring roll wrappers
- 1 cup shredded cabbage
- 1 cup grated carrots
- 1/2 cup bean sprouts
- 1/2 cup finely chopped mushrooms
- 2 green onions, thinly sliced
- 1 garlic clove, minced
- 1 tablespoon soy sauce
- 1 teaspoon sesame oil
- 1/2 teaspoon grated ginger
- 1/2 teaspoon sugar
- 1/4 teaspoon salt
- 1/4 teaspoon black pepper
- Cooking spray or oil for brushing

1. Preheat your air fryer to 375°F (190°C) for about 5 minutes.
2. In a mixing bowl, combine the shredded cabbage, grated carrots, bean sprouts, mushrooms, green onions, minced garlic, soy sauce, sesame oil, grated ginger, sugar, salt, and black pepper. Toss the mixture until all the ingredients are well combined.
3. Lay a spring roll wrapper on a clean work surface, positioning it in a diamond shape. Spoon approximately 2 tablespoons of the vegetable filling onto the bottom corner of the wrapper.
4. Fold the bottom corner over the filling, then fold in the two side corners. Roll the wrapper tightly, sealing the top corner with a bit of water to secure the spring roll. Repeat this process with the remaining wrappers and filling.
5. Lightly coat the spring rolls with cooking spray or brush them with a small amount of oil to promote browning and crispiness.
6. Place the spring rolls in the air fryer basket, making sure they are not touching each other. You may need to cook them in batches if your air fryer is smaller.
7. Air fry the spring rolls at 375°F (190°C) for 8-10 minutes, or until they turn golden brown and crispy, flipping them halfway through.
8. Once cooked, remove the spring rolls from the air fryer and let them cool slightly before serving.
9. Serve the crispy air fried spring rolls with your favorite dipping sauce.

3. SWEET AND SOUR CHICKEN

Ingredients

- 2 boneless, skinless chicken breasts, cut into bite-sized pieces
- 1/4 cup (60 ml) ketchup
- 2 tablespoons (30 ml) rice vinegar
- 2 tablespoons (30 ml) honey
- 1 tablespoon (15 ml) soy sauce
- 1 teaspoon (5 ml) grated fresh ginger
- 1 clove garlic, minced
- 1/4 teaspoon (1.25 ml) red pepper flakes (optional)
- 1/4 cup (30 g) all-purpose flour
- 1/4 cup (30 g) cornstarch
- 1/2 teaspoon (2.5 ml) salt
- 1/4 teaspoon (1.25 ml) black pepper
- Vegetable oil cooking spray
- Chopped green onions and sesame seeds for garnish

1. In a bowl, whisk together the ketchup, rice vinegar, honey, soy sauce, grated ginger, minced garlic, and red pepper flakes (if using). Set aside.
2. In a separate bowl, combine the all-purpose flour, cornstarch, salt, and black pepper. Stir well to ensure the dry ingredients are evenly mixed.
3. Preheat your air fryer to 400°F (200°C).
4. Toss the chicken pieces into the flour mixture, coating them thoroughly. Shake off any excess flour.
5. Lightly coat the air fryer basket with vegetable oil cooking spray to prevent sticking.
6. Place the coated chicken pieces in a single layer in the air fryer basket, leaving a little space between each piece.
7. Air fry the chicken at 400°F (200°C) for 10 minutes, flipping the pieces halfway through the cooking time to ensure even browning.
8. After 10 minutes, carefully remove the chicken from the air fryer.
9. In a large skillet over medium heat, pour the sweet and sour sauce mixture. Heat it gently until it thickens slightly, stirring constantly.
10. Add the air-fried chicken to the skillet and toss it in the sauce, ensuring that each piece is evenly coated.
11. Cook for an additional 2-3 minutes, until the chicken is fully cooked and the sauce has thickened and glazed the pieces.
12. Transfer the Sweet and Sour Chicken to a serving dish, and garnish with chopped green onions and sesame seeds for an extra touch of flavor and visual appeal.

4. ORANGE CHICKEN

Ingredients

- 1 lb (450g) boneless, skinless chicken thighs, cut into bite-sized pieces
- 1/4 cup (60ml) freshly squeezed orange juice
- 2 tablespoons soy sauce
- 2 tablespoons honey
- 1 tablespoon orange zest
- 1 teaspoon grated fresh ginger
- 1/2 teaspoon garlic powder
- 1/4 teaspoon red pepper flakes (adjust to your spice preference)
- 1/2 cup (60g) all-purpose flour
- 1/2 cup (60g) cornstarch
- Salt and pepper, to taste
- Cooking spray or oil mister

1. Preheat your air fryer to 375°F (190°C).
2. In a medium bowl, whisk together the orange juice, soy sauce, honey, orange zest, grated ginger, garlic powder, and red pepper flakes to make the orange glaze.
3. In a separate bowl, combine the all-purpose flour, cornstarch, salt, and pepper to create the coating mixture.
4. Dip each piece of chicken into the coating mixture, making sure to coat it evenly. Shake off any excess flour.
5. Place the coated chicken pieces in the air fryer basket in a single layer. You may need to cook the chicken in batches to avoid overcrowding.
6. Lightly spray or mist the chicken pieces with cooking spray or oil to help achieve a crispy texture.
7. Air fry the chicken at 375°F (190°C) for 10-12 minutes, flipping the pieces halfway through to ensure even cooking. The chicken should turn golden brown and crispy.
8. Once the chicken is cooked, transfer it to a plate and let it rest for a minute.
9. Drizzle the prepared orange glaze over the crispy air-fried chicken and toss gently to coat each piece with the flavorful sauce.
10. Serve the Crispy Air Fried Orange Chicken with steamed jasmine rice or noodles, and garnish with sesame seeds and green onions for an extra touch of freshness and aroma.

Enjoy the vibrant flavors of this Crispy Air Fried Orange Chicken, a delightful twist on a classic Chinese favorite, made effortlessly in your air fryer. A burst of citrusy zest with tender, crispy chicken will make this meal a highlight for your dinner table.

5. CRISPY KUNG PAO SHRIMP

Ingredients

- 12 large shrimp, peeled and deveined
- 1 tablespoon cornstarch
- 1 tablespoon water
- 2 tablespoons vegetable oil
- 2 garlic cloves, minced
- 1 teaspoon fresh ginger, grated
- 2 green onions, sliced (both white and green parts)
- 1/4 cup unsalted peanuts
- 2 tablespoons soy sauce
- 1 tablespoon rice vinegar
- 1 tablespoon hoisin sauce
- 1 tablespoon honey
- 1/2 teaspoon chili flakes (adjust to your preferred spice level)
- 1/2 teaspoon toasted sesame oil
- Zest and juice of 1 small lime
- Fresh cilantro leaves, for garnish

1. Preheat your air fryer to 400°F (200°C).
2. In a small bowl, mix the cornstarch and water to form a smooth slurry.
3. Toss the peeled and deveined shrimp in the cornstarch slurry, ensuring they are evenly coated.
4. Place the coated shrimp in a single layer in the air fryer basket, ensuring they have space between them for even cooking.
5. Air fry the shrimp for 5 minutes until they turn golden and crispy. Shake the basket halfway through cooking to ensure even browning.
6. While the shrimp are air frying, prepare the Kung Pao sauce in a separate bowl. Combine soy sauce, rice vinegar, hoisin sauce, honey, chili flakes, toasted sesame oil, lime zest, and lime juice. Mix well and set aside.
7. In a skillet or frying pan, heat vegetable oil over medium-high heat. Add minced garlic, grated ginger, and sliced green onions (white parts). Sauté for about 1 minute until aromatic.
8. Add the air-fried shrimp to the skillet, along with the Kung Pao sauce and unsalted peanuts. Toss everything together until the shrimp are well coated with the sauce and heated through.
9. Transfer the Kung Pao shrimp to a serving dish, garnish with the sliced green parts of the green onions and fresh cilantro leaves.
10. Serve immediately over steamed rice and enjoy the crispy, spicy, and flavorful delight of this Air Fried Kung Pao Shrimp!

Adjust the spiciness and sweetness of the sauce according to your preference. Serve with additional lime wedges on the side for an extra zesty kick.

6. GENERAL TSO'S CHICKEN

Ingredients

- 1 lb (450g) boneless, skinless chicken thighs, cut into bite-sized pieces
- 1/4 cup (60ml) soy sauce
- 2 tablespoons hoisin sauce
- 1 tablespoon rice vinegar
- 1 tablespoon honey
- 1 tablespoon sesame oil
- 2 cloves garlic, minced
- 1 teaspoon fresh ginger, grated
- 1/2 teaspoon red pepper flakes (adjust to your desired spice level)
- 1/4 cup (30g) cornstarch
- 1/4 cup (30g) all-purpose flour
- Cooking spray or oil mister
- 1 tablespoon sesame seeds, for garnish (optional)
- Sliced scallions, for garnish

1. Preheat your air fryer to 390°F (200°C).
2. In a bowl, combine the soy sauce, hoisin sauce, rice vinegar, honey, sesame oil, minced garlic, grated ginger, and red pepper flakes. Mix the sauce until well combined.
3. In a separate bowl, toss the bite-sized chicken pieces with cornstarch and all-purpose flour until they are evenly coated.
4. Place the coated chicken pieces in the air fryer basket, making sure they are not touching each other to allow for even cooking. You may need to cook in batches if your air fryer is small.
5. Lightly spray the coated chicken pieces with cooking spray or use an oil mister to coat them with a thin layer of oil. This will help achieve a crispy texture.
6. Air fry the chicken at 390°F (200°C) for 15-18 minutes, flipping the pieces halfway through the cooking time to ensure even browning.
7. While the chicken is air frying, take the remaining sauce mixture and heat it in a small saucepan over low heat, stirring occasionally, until it thickens slightly to form a glaze.
8. Once the chicken pieces are perfectly golden and crispy, remove them from the air fryer and toss them in the glaze until they are fully coated.
9. To serve, transfer the General Tso's Chicken to a serving dish, and if desired, sprinkle sesame seeds and sliced scallions on top for a touch of elegance.
10. Enjoy your delectable Air-Fried General Tso's Chicken alongside steamed rice or noodles for a delightful Chinese-inspired feast with your loved one.

7. CRISPY HONEY SESAME CHICKEN

Ingredients

- 1 lb (450g) boneless, skinless chicken thighs, cut into bite-sized pieces
- 2 tablespoons soy sauce
- 1 tablespoon honey
- 1 tablespoon hoisin sauce
- 1 tablespoon rice vinegar
- 1 teaspoon sesame oil
- 1 teaspoon grated fresh ginger
- 2 cloves garlic, minced
- 1/4 teaspoon red pepper flakes (optional, for added heat)
- 2 tablespoons cornstarch
- 2 tablespoons all-purpose flour
- Cooking spray (or oil mister) for greasing the air fryer basket
- 1 tablespoon sesame seeds
- Sliced green onions, for garnish

1. Preheat your air fryer to 380°F (193°C).
2. In a mixing bowl, combine soy sauce, honey, hoisin sauce, rice vinegar, sesame oil, grated ginger, minced garlic, and red pepper flakes (if using). Whisk the marinade until well blended.
3. Add the chicken pieces to the marinade and toss them to coat evenly. Allow the chicken to marinate for at least 15 minutes to absorb the flavors.
4. In a separate shallow dish, combine cornstarch and all-purpose flour. Dredge each marinated chicken piece in the flour mixture, shaking off any excess.
5. Lightly grease the air fryer basket with cooking spray or an oil mister to prevent sticking.
6. Arrange the coated chicken pieces in a single layer in the air fryer basket, making sure they don't overlap.
7. Air fry the chicken at 380°F (193°C) for 12-15 minutes, flipping the pieces halfway through the cooking time. The chicken should be golden brown and crispy on the outside, and thoroughly cooked on the inside.
8. Once cooked, transfer the honey sesame chicken to a serving plate, and sprinkle with sesame seeds.
9. Garnish with sliced green onions for a fresh touch.
10. Serve the Crispy Air Fried Honey Sesame Chicken immediately with steamed rice or your favorite side dishes.

8. SWEET AND SPICY BEEF

Ingredients

- 12 oz (340g) beef sirloin, thinly sliced
- 2 tablespoons soy sauce
- 1 tablespoon hoisin sauce
- 1 tablespoon honey
- 1 teaspoon rice vinegar
- 1/2 teaspoon chili flakes (adjust to your spice preference)
- 1/2 teaspoon garlic powder
- 1/4 teaspoon ground ginger
- 1/4 teaspoon black pepper
- 1 tablespoon cornstarch
- 1 tablespoon water
- 1 tablespoon vegetable oil
- Fresh cilantro or green onions, for garnish

1. Preheat the air fryer to 400°F (200°C).
2. Prepare the beef: In a mixing bowl, combine the soy sauce, hoisin sauce, honey, rice vinegar, chili flakes, garlic powder, ground ginger, and black pepper. Mix well to create a sweet and spicy glaze.
3. Coat the beef: Toss the sliced beef in the glaze, ensuring each piece is evenly coated. Let it marinate for about 10 minutes, allowing the flavors to infuse.
4. Create the cornstarch slurry: In a separate small bowl, whisk together the cornstarch and water to form a slurry.
5. Air fry the beef: Drizzle the vegetable oil over the marinated beef, giving it a glossy sheen. Place the beef in a single layer in the air fryer basket, ensuring there is space between the slices to promote crispiness.
6. Cook in batches: Depending on the size of your air fryer, you might need to cook the beef in batches to avoid overcrowding. Fry each batch for 8-10 minutes, flipping the beef halfway through the cooking time for even crispness.
7. Brush with cornstarch slurry: Midway through cooking, open the air fryer and brush the beef slices with the cornstarch slurry, giving them an extra crispy texture.
8. Serve and garnish: Once the beef is golden brown and crispy, remove it from the air fryer. Garnish with fresh cilantro or chopped green onions for a burst of freshness.
9. Serve and enjoy: Plate the crispy sweet and spicy beef, ready to be served with steamed jasmine rice and your favorite stir-fried vegetables for a delightful meal.

9. SALT AND PEPPER TOFU

Ingredients

- 8 oz (227g) firm tofu, drained and cubed
- 1 tablespoon cornstarch
- 1/2 teaspoon sea salt
- 1/2 teaspoon ground black pepper
- 1/4 teaspoon Chinese five-spice powder
- 1/4 teaspoon garlic powder
- 1/4 teaspoon onion powder
- 1/4 teaspoon red pepper flakes (optional, for added heat)
- 1 tablespoon vegetable oil
- Fresh cilantro leaves, for garnish
- Sliced green onions, for garnish
- Lime wedges, for serving

1. Preheat the Air Fryer: Start by preheating your air fryer to 400°F (200°C) for 5 minutes. This will ensure the perfect crispiness of the tofu.
2. Prepare the Tofu: While the air fryer is heating up, take the firm tofu and drain any excess water. Pat the tofu dry with paper towels, then cut it into bite-sized cubes.
3. Coat the Tofu: In a bowl, combine cornstarch, sea salt, black pepper, Chinese five-spice powder, garlic powder, and onion powder. Toss the tofu cubes in the spice mixture until they are evenly coated.
4. Prep the Air Fryer Basket: Lightly grease the air fryer basket with vegetable oil to prevent sticking. Place the seasoned tofu cubes in a single layer in the basket.
5. Air Fry the Tofu: Slide the basket into the preheated air fryer. Cook the tofu at 400°F (200°C) for 15-18 minutes, flipping the tofu halfway through the cooking time for even browning. The tofu should turn golden brown and crispy on all sides.
6. Serve: Once the tofu is perfectly crispy, transfer it to a serving dish. Garnish with fresh cilantro leaves and sliced green onions for a burst of color and flavor. Serve the salt and pepper tofu immediately with lime wedges on the side for a zesty touch.

10. SZECHUAN EGGPLANT

Ingredients

- 2 small Chinese eggplants, cut into bite-sized pieces
- 2 tablespoons vegetable oil
- 2 tablespoons soy sauce
- 1 tablespoon rice vinegar
- 1 tablespoon hoisin sauce
- 1 tablespoon Szechuan sauce (adjust to taste for desired spiciness)
- 1 teaspoon honey (or maple syrup for a vegan option)
- 1 garlic clove, minced
- 1 teaspoon grated ginger
- 1 tablespoon cornstarch
- 1 tablespoon water
- 2 green onions, sliced (for garnish)
- Sesame seeds (for garnish)

1. Preheat your air fryer to 380°F (193°C).
2. In a mixing bowl, whisk together soy sauce, rice vinegar, hoisin sauce, Szechuan sauce, honey, minced garlic, and grated ginger, forming a well-combined sauce.
3. In a separate small bowl, create a slurry by mixing cornstarch and water until smooth.
4. Toss the eggplant pieces in the vegetable oil until evenly coated.
5. Place the oil-coated eggplant into the preheated air fryer basket, ensuring they are arranged in a single layer to allow even cooking.
6. Air fry the eggplant at 380°F (193°C) for 5 minutes, then carefully flip the pieces and air fry for an additional 5 minutes until they become tender and slightly crispy.
7. Remove the air-fried eggplant from the air fryer and transfer it to a plate.
8. In a saucepan over medium heat, pour the prepared sauce and bring it to a gentle simmer.
9. Add the cornstarch slurry to the simmering sauce, stirring constantly until it thickens and coats the back of a spoon.
10. Pour the thickened Szechuan sauce over the air-fried eggplant, tossing gently to ensure each piece is well coated.
11. Serve the Air Fried Szechuan Eggplant on a platter, garnishing it with sliced green onions and a sprinkle of sesame seeds for an extra touch of flavor and presentation.
12. Enjoy the explosive Szechuan flavors with steamed rice or noodles, and relish the wonderful blend of spice, tang, and smoky notes in this delightful dish!

11. TERIYAKI SALMON

Ingredients

- 2 salmon fillets (approximately 6 ounces each) [2 salmon fillets (170g each)]
- 1/4 cup soy sauce
- 1/4 cup mirin
- 1 tablespoon rice vinegar
- 2 tablespoons brown sugar
- 1 teaspoon grated fresh ginger
- 1 teaspoon grated garlic
- 1 tablespoon sesame oil
- 1 tablespoon sesame seeds, for garnish
- Sliced green onions, for garnish
- Steamed white rice, to serve

1. Begin by preparing the teriyaki marinade. In a bowl, combine the soy sauce, mirin, rice vinegar, brown sugar, grated ginger, and grated garlic. Whisk the mixture until the sugar dissolves completely, creating a velvety-smooth teriyaki sauce.
2. Place the salmon fillets in a shallow dish or a resealable plastic bag, ensuring they have enough space to be coated by the marinade. Pour the teriyaki sauce over the salmon, making sure the fillets are thoroughly covered. Seal the bag or cover the dish and refrigerate for at least 30 minutes.
3. Preheat your air fryer to 375°F (190°C) for 5 minutes, ensuring it reaches the optimal temperature for cooking the salmon to perfection.
4. Once the marinating time is complete, remove the salmon from the marinade, reserving the excess sauce for later use. Pat the fillets dry with a paper towel, ensuring a better sear and preventing excess moisture during cooking.
5. Lightly brush the air fryer basket or tray with sesame oil to prevent sticking. Place the salmon fillets in the basket or on the tray, ensuring they are evenly spaced.
6. Air fry the salmon at 375°F (190°C) for 8-10 minutes or until the salmon reaches your desired level of doneness. The cooking time may vary depending on the thickness of the fillets. For a succulent and flaky texture, avoid overcooking.
7. While the salmon cooks, take the reserved teriyaki sauce and pour it into a small saucepan. Bring the sauce to a gentle simmer over medium heat, stirring occasionally, until it thickens to a glaze-like consistency.
8. Once the salmon is ready, remove it from the air fryer and transfer it to a serving plate. Drizzle the luscious teriyaki glaze over the salmon fillets, letting the flavors harmonize effortlessly.
9. Sprinkle the salmon with sesame seeds and sliced green onions for an enticing touch of garnish.

12. CRISPY FIVE-SPICE RIBS

Ingredients

- 1 lb (450g) pork ribs, cut into individual pieces
- 1 tablespoon vegetable oil
- 1 teaspoon Chinese five-spice powder
- 1 teaspoon garlic powder
- 1 teaspoon onion powder
- 1/2 teaspoon ground ginger
- 1 tablespoon soy sauce
- 1 tablespoon hoisin sauce
- 1 tablespoon honey
- 1 tablespoon rice vinegar
- Salt and pepper, to taste
- Fresh cilantro leaves, for garnish

1. Preheat the Air Fryer: Set your air fryer to 400°F (200°C) and allow it to preheat while you prepare the ribs.
2. Prepare the Ribs: Pat the ribs dry with a paper towel to remove excess moisture. This will help the spices adhere better to the meat.
3. Create the Spice Rub: In a small bowl, combine the Chinese five-spice powder, garlic powder, onion powder, ground ginger, salt, and pepper.
4. Season the Ribs: Rub the spice mixture generously all over the ribs, ensuring each piece is evenly coated.
5. Air Fry the Ribs (First Round): Lightly grease the air fryer basket with vegetable oil. Place the seasoned ribs in a single layer in the basket, making sure they don't overlap. Air fry for 15 minutes, flipping the ribs halfway through the cooking time for even browning.
6. Prepare the Glaze: While the ribs are cooking, mix the soy sauce, hoisin sauce, honey, and rice vinegar in a small bowl to create the glaze.
7. Coat the Ribs with Glaze: After the initial 15 minutes, remove the ribs from the air fryer. Brush each rib with the prepared glaze, making sure to coat all sides thoroughly.
8. Air Fry the Ribs (Second Round): Place the glazed ribs back in the air fryer, and air fry for an additional 5-8 minutes or until the ribs are beautifully caramelized and crisp.
9. Serve and Garnish: Once cooked to perfection, transfer the Five-Spice Ribs to a serving platter. Sprinkle fresh cilantro leaves on top for a burst of color and flavor.
10. Bon Appétit: Dive into the delightful crispy goodness of these Five-Spice Ribs with your loved one and savor the harmonious blend of Chinese spices that elevate this classic dish to new heights.

13. SOY GINGER GLAZED WINGS

Ingredients

- 10 chicken wings, tips removed (for a more luxurious option, use free-range wings)
- 2 tablespoons soy sauce
- 1 tablespoon fresh ginger, grated
- 1 tablespoon honey (or maple syrup for a vegan alternative)
- 1 tablespoon rice vinegar
- 1 teaspoon sesame oil
- 1 teaspoon garlic powder
- 1/4 teaspoon red pepper flakes (adjust to your desired level of spiciness)
- Pinch of salt
- Freshly ground black pepper, to taste
- Sesame seeds and chopped green onions, for garnish

1. Preheat your air fryer to 400°F (200°C) to ensure the wings cook evenly and become delightfully crispy.
2. In a large mixing bowl, combine the soy sauce, grated ginger, honey, rice vinegar, sesame oil, garlic powder, red pepper flakes, salt, and black pepper. Give everything a good mix until the marinade is well combined.
3. Add the chicken wings to the bowl, ensuring they are thoroughly coated with the fragrant marinade. Allow the wings to marinate for at least 30 minutes, or for an intensified flavor, let them rest for a couple of hours in the refrigerator.
4. Line the air fryer basket with parchment paper or lightly brush it with oil to prevent sticking.
5. Place the marinated wings in a single layer in the air fryer basket. Make sure to leave some space between the wings to ensure they cook evenly and turn crispy all over.
6. Air fry the wings at 400°F (200°C) for 20-25 minutes, flipping them halfway through the cooking time. Keep a watchful eye to avoid overcooking, as air fryer models may vary slightly in temperature and power.
7. Once the wings are done, transfer them to a serving plate and sprinkle them with sesame seeds and chopped green onions for an enticing touch.
8. These delectable Air Fried Soy Ginger Glazed Wings are now ready to be savored! Serve them piping hot with your favorite dipping sauce or alongside a refreshing salad for a delightful dining experience.

14. CRISPY BEEF AND BROCCOLI

Ingredients

- 1/2 pound (225g) beef sirloin, thinly sliced
- 1 cup broccoli florets
- 2 tablespoons cornstarch
- 1/4 cup low-sodium soy sauce
- 2 tablespoons hoisin sauce
- 1 tablespoon oyster sauce
- 1 tablespoon brown sugar
- 2 teaspoons grated fresh ginger
- 2 teaspoons minced garlic
- 1/4 teaspoon red pepper flakes (optional)
- 1 tablespoon vegetable oil
- Sesame seeds and sliced green onions for garnish

1. Preheat the Air Fryer: Preheat your air fryer to 400°F (200°C).
2. Coat Beef with Cornstarch: In a medium bowl, combine the sliced beef and cornstarch. Toss until the beef is evenly coated with the cornstarch.
3. Prepare the Sauce: In another bowl, whisk together the soy sauce, hoisin sauce, oyster sauce, brown sugar, grated ginger, minced garlic, and red pepper flakes (if using). Set the sauce aside.
4. Air Fry the Beef: Drizzle the vegetable oil over the cornstarch-coated beef slices and toss to coat. Place the beef in a single layer in the air fryer basket, making sure they don't overlap. Cook the beef in the air fryer for 6-8 minutes, flipping halfway through, until the beef turns crispy and golden brown.
5. Cook the Broccoli: While the beef is air frying, blanch the broccoli florets in boiling water for 2 minutes. Drain and set aside.
6. Combine Beef, Broccoli, and Sauce: Once the beef is crispy, remove it from the air fryer basket and set it aside. Place the blanched broccoli in the air fryer basket, then pour the prepared sauce over the broccoli. Gently toss to coat the broccoli in the sauce.
7. Air Fry the Beef and Broccoli Together: Return the crispy beef to the air fryer basket alongside the sauced broccoli. Cook for an additional 2-3 minutes to allow the flavors to meld and the sauce to thicken slightly.
8. Serve and Garnish: Transfer the air-fried beef and broccoli to a serving plate. Sprinkle with sesame seeds and sliced green onions for a final touch of flavor and presentation.
9. Enjoy: Serve the Air Fryer Crispy Beef and Broccoli over steamed rice or noodles, and enjoy this delightful Chinese-style meal with your loved one!

15. CRISPY FRIED SWEET CHILI SHRIMP

Ingredients

- 2 tablespoons cornstarch
- 1 tablespoon all-purpose flour
- 1/2 teaspoon baking powder
- 1/4 teaspoon salt
- 1/4 teaspoon black pepper
- 1 large egg, beaten
- 1/4 cup sweet chili sauce
- 1 tablespoon soy sauce
- 1 teaspoon sesame oil
- 1 tablespoon lime juice
- 1/2 teaspoon grated ginger
- 2 garlic cloves, minced
- 1/4 cup sliced scallions, for garnish
- 1 tablespoon toasted sesame seeds, for garnish

1. Preheat Air Fryer: Preheat your air fryer to 400°F (200°C) for 5 minutes, ensuring it's thoroughly heated and ready for our culinary adventure.
2. Prepare Shrimp: In a shallow bowl, mix cornstarch, flour, baking powder, salt, and black pepper. Toss the peeled and deveined shrimp in the flour mixture, ensuring they are evenly coated.
3. Egg Wash: Dip the flour-coated shrimp into the beaten egg, covering them entirely in a luscious egg wash, which will create that irresistible crunch.
4. Sweet Chili Glaze: In another bowl, combine sweet chili sauce, soy sauce, sesame oil, lime juice, grated ginger, and minced garlic. Whisk it into a harmonious blend of sweet and spicy flavors.
5. Glaze the Shrimp: Gently coat the egg-washed shrimp with the sweet chili glaze, making sure each piece is beautifully coated with the mouthwatering sauce.
6. Air Frying: Carefully place the glazed shrimp in the preheated air fryer basket, ensuring they are not touching each other to allow even cooking. Air fry for 8-10 minutes, flipping them halfway through, until they turn gloriously golden brown and crispy.
7. Garnish and Serve: Once the shrimp is cooked to perfection, transfer them to a serving plate. Sprinkle sliced scallions and toasted sesame seeds over the top for a delightful burst of color and aroma. Serve these delectable Crispy Air Fried Sweet Chili Shrimp as an appetizer or with steamed rice for a delightful main course.

16. HONEY GARLIC PORK CHOPS

Ingredients

- 2 bone-in pork chops (about 1 inch thick each)
- 3 tablespoons (44 ml) honey
- 2 tablespoons (30 ml) soy sauce
- 2 cloves garlic, minced
- 1 tablespoon (15 ml) rice vinegar
- 1 teaspoon (5 ml) sesame oil
- 1/2 teaspoon (2.5 ml) ground ginger
- Pinch of black pepper
- Fresh cilantro leaves, for garnish (optional)
- Toasted sesame seeds, for garnish (optional)
- Steamed rice and steamed broccoli, to serve

1. In a small bowl, whisk together the honey, soy sauce, minced garlic, rice vinegar, sesame oil, ground ginger, and a pinch of black pepper. This tantalizing marinade is the heart of our flavorful pork chops.

2. Place the pork chops in a shallow dish and pour half of the marinade over them, ensuring they are thoroughly coated. Cover the dish with plastic wrap and let the chops marinate in the refrigerator for at least 30 minutes. Meanwhile, let the remaining marinade rest at room temperature.

3. Preheat your air fryer to 400°F (200°C). Allow the air fryer to reach the desired temperature while you relish the anticipation of the delightful feast ahead.

4. Once the pork chops have marinated, remove them from the dish, allowing any excess marinade to drip off. Set the pork chops aside on a plate.

5. Place the marinated pork chops in the preheated air fryer basket, making sure they are not touching each other to allow even cooking. Cook the pork chops in the air fryer for 12-15 minutes, flipping them halfway through the cooking time. The chops should be gloriously golden and cooked to juicy perfection.

6. While the pork chops are air frying, take the reserved marinade and transfer it to a small saucepan. Bring the marinade to a gentle boil over medium heat, then reduce the heat and let it simmer for 2-3 minutes until slightly thickened. This will become a glossy glaze that amplifies the flavors of our succulent pork chops.

7. Once the pork chops are done, remove them from the air fryer and brush both sides generously with the honey garlic glaze. Allow the glaze to set for a minute, further enhancing the tantalizing taste.

8. To serve, garnish the Air Fried Honey Garlic Pork Chops with fresh cilantro leaves and toasted sesame seeds if desired. Present them alongside steamed rice and steamed broccoli for a complete and balanced meal.

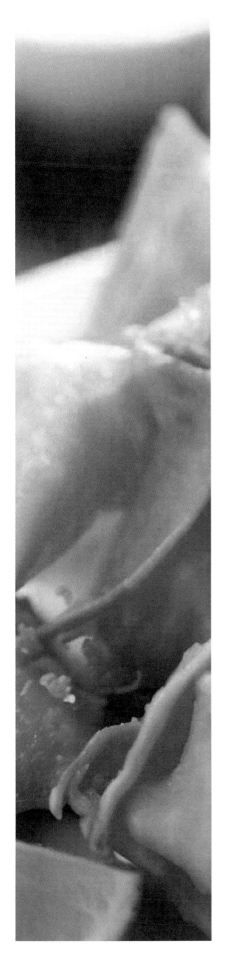

17. FRIED MAPO TOFU

Ingredients

- 10 oz (280g) silken tofu, cubed
- 2 tbsp vegetable oil
- 1/2 lb (225g) ground pork
- 2 garlic cloves, minced
- 1-inch (2.5cm) piece of ginger, grated
- 2 tbsp doubanjiang (spicy bean paste)
- 1 tbsp soy sauce
- 1 tbsp Shaoxing wine (Chinese rice wine)
- 1 tsp Szechuan peppercorns, toasted and ground
- 1 cup (240ml) chicken or vegetable broth
- 1 tsp cornstarch, mixed with 2 tbsp water
- 2 green onions, thinly sliced (for garnish)
- Steamed rice, for serving

1. Preheat your air fryer to 380°F (193°C).
2. Gently pat the cubed tofu with a paper towel to remove excess moisture.
3. In a large skillet over medium-high heat, add 1 tablespoon of vegetable oil and sauté the ground pork until it's no longer pink, breaking it apart with a spoon as it cooks. Remove the cooked pork from the skillet and set it aside.
4. In the same skillet, add the remaining 1 tablespoon of vegetable oil. Stir in the minced garlic and grated ginger, cooking for about 1 minute until fragrant.
5. Lower the heat to medium and stir in the doubanjiang, soy sauce, Shaoxing wine, and ground Szechuan peppercorns. Cook the mixture for another minute, allowing the flavors to meld together.
6. Return the cooked ground pork to the skillet and mix it with the spicy sauce.
7. Gently fold in the cubed tofu, being careful not to break it apart. Let the tofu soak up the flavorful sauce for a minute or two.
8. Transfer the tofu and pork mixture into the air fryer basket, spreading it out evenly.
9. Pour the chicken or vegetable broth into the air fryer basket, making sure it surrounds the tofu and pork mixture.
10. Air fry the Mapo Tofu at 380°F (193°C) for 12-15 minutes or until the sauce thickens and the tofu becomes tender.
11. Carefully remove the air fryer basket from the air fryer and drizzle the cornstarch slurry over the tofu and pork. Gently mix to thicken the sauce.
12. Serve the Air Fried Mapo Tofu over steamed rice and garnish with sliced green onions for a touch of freshness and color.

18. CHINESE BBQ PORK BUNS

Ingredients

- 8 small store-bought or homemade Chinese BBQ pork buns
- 1 tablespoon vegetable oil
- 1 tablespoon water

1. Preparation: Preheat your air fryer to 370°F (188°C) for about 5 minutes, ensuring it's well-heated for cooking perfection.
2. Lightly Grease: Gently brush the air fryer basket with a thin layer of vegetable oil to prevent sticking.
3. Moisture Enhancement: Lightly dab each BBQ pork bun with water to add a touch of moisture, ensuring a soft texture.
4. Air Fry First Side: Place the prepared BBQ pork buns in the air fryer basket in a single layer, leaving some space between them. Air fry at 370°F (188°C) for 5 minutes until the bottoms turn a delightful golden brown.
5. Flip & Air Fry Second Side: Carefully flip each BBQ pork bun to ensure even cooking. Air fry for an additional 3-4 minutes at the same temperature until the tops also achieve a tempting golden hue.
6. Check for Crispiness: Open the air fryer and inspect the buns to see if they have reached the desired level of crispiness. If needed, you can air fry for another minute or two.
7. Serve & Savor: Remove the Air Fried Chinese BBQ Pork Buns from the air fryer, and let them cool for a moment. Delight in these delectable buns as a delightful meal for two or share them as an appetizing snack with loved ones!

19. CRISPY CRAB RANGOON

Ingredients

- 4 oz (113g) canned crab meat, drained and flaked
- 4 oz (113g) cream cheese, softened
- 2 green onions, finely chopped
- 1 garlic clove, minced
- 1/2 teaspoon Worcestershire sauce
- 1/4 teaspoon soy sauce
- 1/4 teaspoon ground ginger
- 1/4 teaspoon white pepper
- 12 wonton wrappers
- Water, for sealing
- Cooking spray

1. In a mixing bowl, combine the flaked crab meat, softened cream cheese, finely chopped green onions, minced garlic, Worcestershire sauce, soy sauce, ground ginger, and white pepper. Mix the ingredients until well combined, creating a luscious crab and cream cheese filling.
2. Lay out the wonton wrappers on a clean surface. Spoon a teaspoonful of the crab and cream cheese mixture onto the center of each wonton wrapper. Be careful not to overfill to ensure easy sealing.
3. Dip your finger in water and moisten the edges of the wonton wrappers. This will help in sealing the rangoon securely.
4. Gently fold the wonton wrapper over the filling, forming a triangle shape. Press the edges firmly to seal the rangoon. You can use a fork to crimp the edges for a decorative touch.
5. Preheat your air fryer to 375°F (190°C).
6. Lightly coat the air fryer basket with cooking spray to prevent sticking. Arrange the crab rangoon in a single layer in the basket, ensuring they are not touching each other.
7. Air fry the crab rangoon at 375°F (190°C) for 6 to 8 minutes, or until they turn crispy and golden brown. For even cooking, you might need to cook them in batches.
8. Once the crab rangoon are delightfully crisp and irresistible, remove them from the air fryer and transfer to a serving plate.
9. Serve the crispy crab rangoon warm, with your favorite dipping sauce on the side. The delightful contrast of textures and flavors will make this dish an instant hit at your table.
10. Savor the delightful taste of these air-fried crab rangoon with your loved one, and revel in the culinary magic you've created, all thanks to the wonders of the air fryer. Bon appétit!

20. SESAME GINGER CAULIFLOWER

Ingredients

- 1 medium head of cauliflower, cut into florets
- 2 tablespoons (30ml) soy sauce
- 1 tablespoon (15ml) sesame oil
- 1 tablespoon (15ml) rice vinegar
- 1 tablespoon (15ml) honey
- 1 tablespoon (15ml) water
- 2 teaspoons (10ml) grated fresh ginger
- 2 cloves garlic, minced
- 1 tablespoon (15ml) vegetable oil
- 1 tablespoon (10g) sesame seeds
- 1 green onion, thinly sliced (for garnish)
- Salt and pepper, to taste

1. Preheat your air fryer to 380°F (193°C).
2. In a small mixing bowl, whisk together the soy sauce, sesame oil, rice vinegar, honey, water, grated ginger, and minced garlic to create a tantalizing marinade.
3. Place the cauliflower florets in a large resealable bag and pour half of the marinade over them. Seal the bag and gently toss to ensure the cauliflower is evenly coated. Let it marinate for about 10 minutes, allowing the flavors to meld.
4. Brush the air fryer basket with vegetable oil to prevent sticking.
5. Carefully transfer the marinated cauliflower to the air fryer basket in a single layer, reserving the leftover marinade.
6. Air fry the cauliflower at 380°F (193°C) for 12-15 minutes, pausing halfway through to shake the basket and ensure even cooking. The cauliflower should turn golden brown and slightly crispy on the edges.
7. While the cauliflower cooks, heat a small pan over medium-low heat. Add the sesame seeds and toast them until they release their nutty fragrance, stirring frequently to prevent burning. Remove from heat and set aside.
8. In the same pan, pour the reserved marinade and simmer over low heat until it thickens slightly, creating a luscious glaze for the cauliflower.
9. Once the cauliflower is done, transfer it to a serving plate, drizzle the glaze over the top, and sprinkle the toasted sesame seeds generously.
10. Garnish the dish with thinly sliced green onions for a pop of color and freshness.
11. Serve the Sesame Ginger Cauliflower immediately as a delightful side dish or as a main course alongside steamed rice or noodles.

21. CRISPY SALT AND PEPPER SQUID

Ingredients

- 10 ounces (280g) squid tubes, cleaned and sliced into rings
- 1/4 cup (30g) all-purpose flour
- 1/4 cup (30g) cornstarch
- 1 teaspoon sea salt
- 1/2 teaspoon freshly ground black pepper
- 1/4 teaspoon Chinese five-spice powder
- 1/4 teaspoon garlic powder
- 1/4 teaspoon onion powder
- 1/4 teaspoon cayenne pepper (optional, for a kick)
- Cooking spray or oil mister

1. Preheat the Air Fryer: Preheat your air fryer to 400°F (200°C) while you prepare the squid.
2. Combine Dry Ingredients: In a shallow dish, mix the all-purpose flour, cornstarch, sea salt, black pepper, Chinese five-spice powder, garlic powder, onion powder, and cayenne pepper (if using). Give the mixture a gentle stir to ensure the spices are evenly distributed.
3. Coat the Squid: Pat the squid rings dry with a paper towel. Working in batches, place the squid rings into the flour mixture and toss them gently to coat them thoroughly with the seasoned flour.
4. Shake Off Excess Flour: Lift the coated squid rings from the flour mixture and shake off any excess before transferring them to a plate. This step ensures a lighter, crisper coating.
5. Prep the Air Fryer Basket: Lightly grease the air fryer basket with cooking spray or use an oil mister to coat it. This helps prevent the squid from sticking and ensures an even cook.
6. Air Fry the Squid: Arrange the coated squid rings in a single layer in the air fryer basket. Avoid overcrowding to ensure proper air circulation and even cooking. Cook in batches if needed. Lightly spray the squid with cooking spray or oil.
7. Air Fry First Side: Place the basket in the preheated air fryer and cook the squid for 5 minutes, or until they turn golden brown and crispy. Give the basket a shake halfway through the cooking time for even browning.
8. Flip and Cook Second Side: Carefully flip the squid rings using tongs or a spatula and air fry for an additional 3-4 minutes, or until the other side becomes golden and crispy as well.

22. ORANGE GLAZED TOFU

Ingredients

- 14 oz (400g) firm tofu, drained and pressed
- 1/4 cup orange juice (60ml)
- 2 tablespoons soy sauce
- 2 tablespoons maple syrup
- 1 teaspoon grated fresh ginger
- 1 garlic clove, minced
- 1/2 teaspoon sesame oil
- 1 tablespoon cornstarch
- 1/4 cup all-purpose flour
- Pinch of salt and pepper
- Sesame seeds, for garnish
- Sliced scallions, for garnish

1. Preparation: Begin by draining the tofu and wrapping it in a clean kitchen towel or paper towels. Place a weight on top to press out excess moisture for about 20 minutes.
2. Orange Glaze: In a small bowl, mix together the orange juice, soy sauce, maple syrup, grated ginger, minced garlic, and sesame oil. Set the glaze aside.
3. Tofu Coating: Cut the pressed tofu into bite-sized cubes. In a shallow dish, combine the cornstarch, all-purpose flour, salt, and pepper. Toss the tofu cubes in the flour mixture, ensuring they are evenly coated.
4. Preheat Air Fryer: Preheat your air fryer to 380°F (193°C).
5. Air Frying: Lightly grease the air fryer basket with cooking spray. Arrange the coated tofu cubes in a single layer in the basket, leaving space between them. Cook in the air fryer for 12-15 minutes, flipping halfway through, until the tofu turns golden brown and crispy.
6. Orange Glazing: Once the tofu is cooked, transfer it to a mixing bowl. Pour the prepared orange glaze over the tofu cubes and gently toss until the glaze evenly coats the tofu.
7. Final Air Frying: Return the glazed tofu to the air fryer basket and cook for an additional 2-3 minutes at 380°F (193°C) to let the glaze caramelize slightly.
8. Serving: Sprinkle the air-fried orange glazed tofu with sesame seeds and sliced scallions for an extra touch of flavor and presentation.
9. Enjoy: Serve the succulent orange-glazed tofu immediately while it's still hot. Pair it with steamed rice and your favorite vegetables for a complete and delectable meal for two.

23. MONGOLIAN BEEF

Ingredients

- 8 ounces (225g) beef sirloin, thinly sliced into strips
- 2 tablespoons cornstarch
- 2 tablespoons vegetable oil
- 2 cloves garlic, minced
- 1/2 teaspoon fresh ginger, grated
- 2 tablespoons soy sauce
- 2 tablespoons water
- 2 tablespoons brown sugar
- 1 teaspoon sesame oil
- 1/4 teaspoon red pepper flakes (optional)
- 2 green onions, sliced, for garnish
- Cooked white rice, to serve

1. Preparation: Pat the beef strips dry with a paper towel to remove any excess moisture. Place the beef in a bowl and toss with the cornstarch until evenly coated.
2. Preheat the Air Fryer: Preheat your air fryer to 400°F (200°C).
3. Sauté Aromatics: In a small saucepan or skillet, heat the vegetable oil over medium heat. Add the minced garlic and grated ginger, and sauté for about 1 minute until fragrant.
4. Prepare the Sauce: To the saucepan, add the soy sauce, water, brown sugar, sesame oil, and red pepper flakes (if using). Stir the sauce until the sugar is dissolved and let it simmer for 2 minutes to thicken slightly.
5. Air Fry the Beef: Place the cornstarch-coated beef strips into the preheated air fryer basket in a single layer. Cook the beef in batches if needed to avoid overcrowding. Air fry the beef for 6-8 minutes, flipping halfway through, until it becomes crispy and caramelized.
6. Combine Beef with Sauce: Once the beef is cooked, transfer it to a large bowl and pour the prepared sauce over it. Toss the beef gently until all the strips are coated in the savory sauce.
7. Garnish and Serve: Serve the delicious Air Fried Mongolian Beef over a bed of cooked white rice. Garnish with sliced green onions for a pop of color and added freshness.

24. GARLIC SOY EDAMAME

Ingredients

- 1 cup frozen edamame, in their pods
- 1 tablespoon soy sauce
- 1 teaspoon sesame oil
- 1 teaspoon vegetable oil
- 2 garlic cloves, minced
- 1/4 teaspoon red pepper flakes (optional)
- 1 tablespoon sesame seeds
- Pinch of salt
- Pinch of black pepper
- Fresh cilantro leaves, for garnish (optional)

1. Preheat your air fryer to 400°F (200°C) for 5 minutes.
2. In a mixing bowl, combine soy sauce, sesame oil, vegetable oil, minced garlic, red pepper flakes (if using), salt, and black pepper. Stir well to create a luscious garlic soy glaze.
3. Add the frozen edamame to the bowl with the glaze, tossing them gently to coat each pod evenly.
4. Transfer the marinated edamame to the air fryer basket, arranging them in a single layer to ensure even cooking.
5. Air fry the edamame at 400°F (200°C) for 10-12 minutes or until they become slightly crispy, shaking the basket halfway through the cooking time to promote uniform crispness.
6. While the edamame cooks, toast the sesame seeds in a dry pan over medium heat until they turn golden brown. Set them aside for garnishing.
7. Once the edamame pods are perfectly air fried, remove them from the air fryer and transfer to a serving bowl.
8. Sprinkle the toasted sesame seeds over the edamame, adding an extra layer of nutty goodness.
9. For a finishing touch, garnish with fresh cilantro leaves if desired, for a burst of freshness.
10. Serve the Air Fried Garlic Soy Edamame immediately and let the bold flavors take center stage. Enjoy this delightful appetizer with your loved ones and embrace the authentic taste of Chinese cuisine.

25. LEMON PEPPER WINGS

Ingredients

- 1 lb (450g) chicken wings, split into drumettes and flats
- 2 tablespoons olive oil
- 1 tablespoon lemon zest
- 1 teaspoon black pepper
- 1/2 teaspoon salt
- 1/2 teaspoon garlic powder
- 1/2 teaspoon onion powder
- 1/4 teaspoon cayenne pepper (optional, for added heat)
- Lemon wedges, for serving

1. Preheat your air fryer to 400°F (200°C) for 5 minutes.
2. In a large bowl, combine the olive oil, lemon zest, black pepper, salt, garlic powder, onion powder, and cayenne pepper (if using). Mix well to create the lemon pepper marinade.
3. Add the chicken wings to the marinade, ensuring they are evenly coated. Allow the wings to marinate for at least 20 minutes to absorb the delicious flavors.
4. Place the marinated wings in the preheated air fryer basket in a single layer, leaving space between each wing to promote even cooking.
5. Air fry the wings at 400°F (200°C) for 20-25 minutes, flipping them halfway through to ensure they cook evenly and achieve that irresistible crispy texture.
6. Once the wings are golden brown and cooked through, remove them from the air fryer and let them rest for a minute.
7. Serve the Air Fried Lemon Pepper Wings on a platter, garnished with fresh lemon wedges for an extra zesty kick.
8. Enjoy these delectable lemon pepper wings as a delightful appetizer or pair them with your favorite sides for a satisfying main course. Remember to savor every bite, as they will surely leave you wanting more.

26. BLACK PEPPER CHICKEN

Ingredients

- 1 lb (450g) boneless, skinless chicken thighs, cut into bite-sized pieces
- 1 tablespoon vegetable oil
- 2 tablespoons dark soy sauce
- 2 tablespoons oyster sauce
- 1 tablespoon Shaoxing wine (Chinese rice wine) [optional]
- 1 tablespoon black peppercorns, coarsely ground
- 2 cloves garlic, minced
- 1-inch piece of fresh ginger, grated
- 1 green bell pepper, sliced
- 1 red bell pepper, sliced
- 2 green onions, sliced (white and green parts separated)
- Steamed white rice, for serving

1. Preheat your air fryer to 400°F (200°C).
2. In a mixing bowl, combine the vegetable oil, dark soy sauce, oyster sauce, Shaoxing wine (if using), and coarsely ground black peppercorns. Stir well to create a flavorful marinade.
3. Add the bite-sized chicken pieces to the marinade, ensuring each piece is well coated. Allow the chicken to marinate for 15-20 minutes, allowing the flavors to meld.
4. Place the marinated chicken in a single layer in the air fryer basket. Reserve any excess marinade.
5. Air fry the chicken at 400°F (200°C) for 10 minutes, then pause and toss the chicken pieces for even cooking. Continue air frying for an additional 5-7 minutes or until the chicken is cooked through and has a lovely golden color.
6. While the chicken is air frying, heat a small saucepan over medium heat. Add the minced garlic and grated ginger, and stir-fry for a minute until fragrant.
7. Pour in the reserved marinade and let it simmer for 2-3 minutes until slightly thickened. Remove the saucepan from heat.
8. Once the chicken is fully cooked, transfer it to a large mixing bowl.
9. In the same air fryer basket, place the sliced green and red bell peppers. Air fry them at 400°F (200°C) for 3-5 minutes until they are slightly tender and charred.
10. Add the air-fried bell peppers to the bowl with the cooked chicken.
11. Drizzle the thickened black pepper sauce over the chicken and peppers. Toss everything together, ensuring the sauce evenly coats the ingredients.
12. Garnish with the sliced green onions' green parts for a fresh burst of flavor and vibrant color.

27. SWEET AND SPICY SHRIMP

Ingredients

- 12 large shrimp, peeled and deveined
- 2 tablespoons soy sauce
- 1 tablespoon honey
- 1 tablespoon sriracha sauce
- 1 teaspoon sesame oil
- 1/2 teaspoon grated fresh ginger
- 1/2 teaspoon minced garlic
- 1/4 teaspoon crushed red pepper flakes (adjust to your spice preference)
- 1 tablespoon chopped green onions (scallions) for garnish
- 1 tablespoon toasted sesame seeds for garnish

1. Preparation: Pat dry the shrimp with a paper towel to remove excess moisture. In a bowl, whisk together soy sauce, honey, sriracha sauce, sesame oil, grated ginger, minced garlic, and crushed red pepper flakes. This divine mixture will be the foundation of our irresistible glaze.

2. Marinating the Shrimp: Place the shrimp in a resealable plastic bag or a shallow dish and pour the marinade over them. Gently toss the shrimp to ensure they are evenly coated with the delectable glaze. Seal the bag or cover the dish with plastic wrap and allow the shrimp to marinate for about 15-20 minutes. This will infuse the flavors and transform the shrimp into a true culinary masterpiece.

3. Preheating the Air Fryer: While the shrimp marinate, preheat your air fryer to 380°F (193°C). A sizzling hot air fryer will ensure that the shrimp cook to a delightful crispiness while retaining their juicy tenderness inside.

4. Arranging the Shrimp: Once the air fryer is preheated, arrange the marinated shrimp in a single layer in the air fryer basket. We want them to have enough space to get beautifully crispy all around.

5. Air Frying the Shrimp: Cook the shrimp in the air fryer for 5-6 minutes, flipping them halfway through. The shrimp should turn a luscious golden color and become slightly caramelized with the sweet and spicy glaze.

6. Garnishing and Serving: Sprinkle the chopped green onions (scallions) and toasted sesame seeds over the succulent shrimp, adding an extra touch of color and flavor. Serve the Sweet and Spicy Shrimp immediately with your favorite side dishes like steamed rice, quinoa, or a refreshing green salad.

7. Now it's time to delight in the divine combination of flavors. Each bite of the Sweet and Spicy Shrimp will be an explosion of taste, leaving you and your dining companion with smiles of satisfaction and contentment.

28. HONEY SRIRACHA WINGS

Ingredients

- 10 chicken wings
- 1/4 cup (60ml) honey
- 2 tablespoons (30ml) sriracha sauce
- 2 tablespoons (30ml) soy sauce
- 1 tablespoon (15ml) rice vinegar
- 1 teaspoon (5ml) sesame oil
- 1/2 teaspoon (2.5ml) garlic powder
- 1/2 teaspoon (2.5ml) onion powder
- 1/2 teaspoon (2.5ml) paprika
- Salt and pepper, to taste
- Fresh cilantro, chopped (for garnish)
- Sesame seeds (for garnish)
- Lime wedges (for serving)

1. Preheat your air fryer to 390°F (200°C).
2. Pat dry the chicken wings with paper towels and place them in a large mixing bowl.
3. In a separate bowl, whisk together the honey, sriracha sauce, soy sauce, rice vinegar, sesame oil, garlic powder, onion powder, and paprika to create a luscious marinade.
4. Pour half of the marinade over the chicken wings, reserving the other half for later. Toss the wings thoroughly to coat them evenly.
5. Let the wings marinate for at least 30 minutes, allowing the flavors to penetrate the meat.
6. Once marinated, arrange the chicken wings in a single layer inside the air fryer basket, making sure they have some space between them for optimal crisping.
7. Air fry the wings for 12-15 minutes, flipping them halfway through the cooking time to ensure even browning.
8. As the wings cook, take the reserved marinade and heat it in a small saucepan until it thickens slightly, creating a luscious glaze.
9. Once the wings are cooked to golden perfection, transfer them to a serving dish.
10. Drizzle the honey sriracha glaze over the wings, allowing the flavors to meld together beautifully.
11. Sprinkle with chopped cilantro and sesame seeds for an added burst of freshness and texture.
12. Serve these delectable Air Fried Honey Sriracha Wings with lime wedges on the side for a tangy touch and enjoy the delightful combination of sweet, spicy, and succulent flavors.

29. GARLIC SESAME GREEN BEANS

Ingredients

- 12 oz (340g) fresh green beans, washed and trimmed
- 2 tablespoons sesame oil
- 2 tablespoons soy sauce
- 2 cloves of garlic, minced
- 1 tablespoon sesame seeds
- 1/4 teaspoon red pepper flakes (optional for a spicy kick)
- Salt and pepper to taste

1. Preheat your air fryer to 400°F (200°C).
2. In a small bowl, mix the sesame oil, soy sauce, minced garlic, and red pepper flakes (if using). Stir well to combine the flavors.
3. Place the washed and trimmed green beans in a mixing bowl and pour the sesame sauce over them. Toss the beans until they are evenly coated in the sauce.
4. Carefully transfer the coated green beans into the air fryer basket, spreading them out in a single layer.
5. Set the air fryer to cook at 400°F (200°C) for 8-10 minutes. Pause the cooking halfway through (around 4 minutes) to shake the basket gently and ensure even cooking.
6. While the green beans are air frying, take a dry skillet over medium heat and toast the sesame seeds until they turn golden and release their nutty aroma. Be sure to keep an eye on them, as they can burn quickly.
7. Once the green beans are done, remove them from the air fryer and place them on a serving platter.
8. Sprinkle the toasted sesame seeds over the green beans, and season with a pinch of salt and pepper to taste.
9. Serve the Air Fried Garlic Sesame Green Beans as a delightful side dish alongside your favorite main course or as a light and flavorful snack.

30. SALT AND PEPPER PORK BELLY

Ingredients

- 1/2 lb (225g) pork belly, skin removed and cut into bite-sized pieces
- 1 tablespoon vegetable oil
- 1 teaspoon sea salt
- 1 teaspoon ground black pepper
- 1/2 teaspoon Chinese five-spice powder
- 1/4 teaspoon garlic powder
- 1/4 teaspoon onion powder
- 1/4 teaspoon chili flakes (optional for added heat)
- Fresh cilantro or green onions, for garnish

1. Preheat your air fryer to 400°F (200°C).
2. In a large bowl, toss the pork belly pieces with vegetable oil until evenly coated.
3. In a separate bowl, mix together the sea salt, ground black pepper, Chinese five-spice powder, garlic powder, onion powder, and chili flakes (if using).
4. Sprinkle the spice mix over the pork belly and toss well, ensuring the spices coat the meat thoroughly.
5. Place the seasoned pork belly pieces in the air fryer basket in a single layer, leaving some space between each piece for even cooking.
6. Air fry the pork belly at 400°F (200°C) for 12-15 minutes, or until the meat is cooked through and the exterior is crispy and golden brown.
7. Gently shake the air fryer basket halfway through the cooking time to ensure even browning.
8. Once cooked, remove the pork belly from the air fryer and transfer to a serving plate.
9. Garnish with fresh cilantro or green onions for an extra touch of flavor and color.
10. Serve the delectable Air Fryer Salt and Pepper Pork Belly immediately, and savor the wonderful blend of textures and aromas.

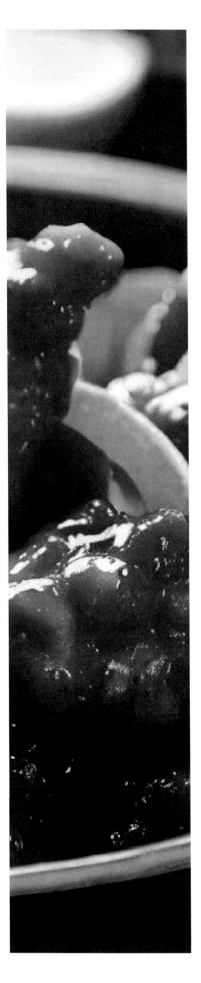

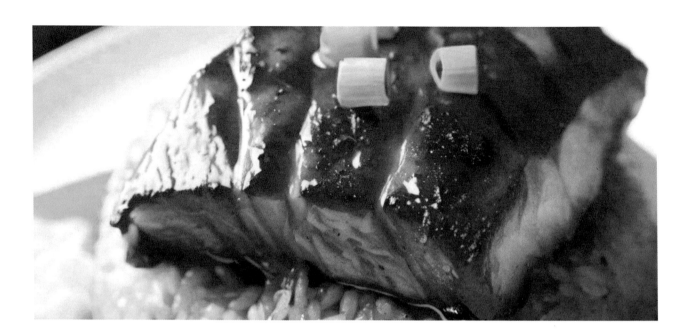

31. FRIED HOISIN GLAZED SALMON

Ingredients

- 2 salmon fillets (6 oz each)
- 2 tablespoons hoisin sauce
- 1 tablespoon soy sauce
- 1 tablespoon honey
- 1 teaspoon sesame oil
- 1 teaspoon grated fresh ginger
- 2 cloves garlic, minced
- 1 tablespoon sesame seeds
- Sliced scallions, for garnish

1. Preheat your air fryer to 375°F (190°C).
2. In a small bowl, whisk together the hoisin sauce, soy sauce, honey, sesame oil, grated ginger, and minced garlic to create the luscious glaze.
3. Place the salmon fillets in a shallow dish and generously brush each fillet with the hoisin glaze, reserving some glaze for basting later.
4. Sprinkle the sesame seeds over the glazed salmon fillets, allowing them to adhere for extra texture and flavor.
5. Carefully transfer the glazed salmon fillets to the preheated air fryer basket, ensuring they are well spaced for even cooking.
6. Air fry the salmon for 10-12 minutes, or until the fish is cooked through and easily flakes with a fork. Halfway through the cooking time, use a pastry brush to baste the salmon with the remaining glaze for an irresistible glossy finish.
7. Once the salmon reaches its delightful flakiness, remove it from the air fryer and transfer to a serving plate.
8. Garnish with sliced scallions, adding a pop of color and freshness to the dish.
9. Serve your Air Fried Hoisin Glazed Salmon alongside steamed rice or your favorite stir-fried vegetables for a delightful Chinese-inspired feast that's sure to impress.

32. SPICY TOFU STIR-FRY

Ingredients

- 7 oz (200g) firm tofu, drained and cubed
- 1 tablespoon vegetable oil
- 1/2 red bell pepper, sliced
- 1/2 green bell pepper, sliced
- 1/2 yellow bell pepper, sliced
- 1/2 cup sliced mushrooms
- 2 green onions, sliced diagonally
- 2 cloves garlic, minced
- 1/2-inch piece ginger, grated
- 1 tablespoon soy sauce
- 1 tablespoon hoisin sauce
- 1 tablespoon rice vinegar
- 1 tablespoon chili garlic sauce (adjust to your spice preference)
- 1 teaspoon toasted sesame oil
- 1 tablespoon sesame seeds, for garnish
- Fresh cilantro leaves, for garnish

1. Preheat your air fryer to 400°F (200°C).
2. Gently pat the tofu dry with paper towels and cut it into bite-sized cubes.
3. In a medium-sized bowl, combine the soy sauce, hoisin sauce, rice vinegar, chili garlic sauce, grated ginger, and minced garlic. Mix well to create the spicy sauce.
4. Heat the vegetable oil in a non-stick skillet over medium-high heat. Add the tofu cubes and cook for 2-3 minutes per side until lightly browned. Remove the tofu from the skillet and set it aside.
5. In the same skillet, add the sliced bell peppers, mushrooms, and green onions. Stir-fry for 3-4 minutes until the vegetables are slightly tender.
6. Pour the prepared spicy sauce over the vegetables and toss to coat evenly. Cook for an additional 2 minutes to let the flavors meld.
7. Transfer the sautéed vegetables to the air fryer basket in a single layer. Air fry for 5-6 minutes, shaking the basket halfway through to ensure even cooking.
8. Once the vegetables are crispy and slightly charred, add the cooked tofu to the air fryer basket. Drizzle with toasted sesame oil and toss everything together gently.
9. Air fry for an additional 2 minutes to let the tofu absorb the flavors of the sauce.
10. Carefully remove the air fryer basket, and transfer the spicy tofu stir-fry to a serving plate.
11. Garnish with sesame seeds and fresh cilantro leaves for an extra burst of color and flavor.
12. Serve the spicy tofu stir-fry immediately with steamed rice or noodles for a mouthwatering and satisfying meal shared with your loved one!

33. CHINESE STYLE SPARE RIBS

Ingredients

- 1 lb (450g) pork spare ribs, cut into individual pieces
- 2 tablespoons soy sauce
- 1 tablespoon hoisin sauce
- 1 tablespoon honey
- 1 tablespoon rice vinegar
- 1 teaspoon Chinese five-spice powder
- 1 teaspoon grated fresh ginger
- 2 garlic cloves, minced
- 1 tablespoon vegetable oil
- Freshly ground black pepper, to taste
- Chopped green onions and sesame seeds for garnish

1. Preheat your air fryer to 400°F (200°C).
2. In a bowl, combine the soy sauce, hoisin sauce, honey, rice vinegar, Chinese five-spice powder, grated ginger, and minced garlic to make the marinade.
3. Season the spare ribs with black pepper and then place them in a resealable plastic bag or a shallow dish.
4. Pour the marinade over the ribs, ensuring they are well-coated. Seal the bag or cover the dish, and let the ribs marinate in the refrigerator for at least 1 hour (or preferably overnight) to infuse the flavors.
5. When ready to cook, remove the spare ribs from the marinade and pat them dry with paper towels. Reserve the marinade for later use.
6. Brush the air fryer basket with vegetable oil to prevent sticking.
7. Arrange the spare ribs in a single layer in the air fryer basket, leaving some space between each piece.
8. Set the air fryer to 400°F (200°C) and cook the ribs for 12-15 minutes, flipping them halfway through the cooking time to ensure even browning.
9. While the ribs cook, pour the reserved marinade into a small saucepan and bring it to a boil over medium heat. Let it simmer for 5 minutes until it thickens slightly into a glaze.
10. Once the spare ribs are done, remove them from the air fryer and brush them with the glaze.
11. Garnish the spare ribs with chopped green onions and sesame seeds for an added touch of flavor and presentation.

34. HONEY MUSTARD CHICKEN

Ingredients

- 2 boneless, skinless chicken breasts
- 2 tablespoons Dijon mustard
- 2 tablespoons honey
- 1 tablespoon olive oil
- 1 teaspoon apple cider vinegar
- 1/2 teaspoon garlic powder
- 1/2 teaspoon onion powder
- 1/2 teaspoon paprika
- Salt and pepper, to taste
- Fresh parsley, for garnish

1. Preheat your air fryer to 375°F (190°C).
2. In a small bowl, whisk together Dijon mustard, honey, olive oil, apple cider vinegar, garlic powder, onion powder, paprika, salt, and pepper until the honey mustard glaze is smooth and well combined.
3. Place the chicken breasts in a separate bowl and drizzle a little olive oil over them. Season with a pinch of salt and pepper on both sides.
4. Generously brush each chicken breast with the honey mustard glaze, making sure to coat them evenly on all sides.
5. Place the glazed chicken breasts in the preheated air fryer basket, making sure they are not touching each other, to allow for even air circulation.
6. Air fry the chicken at 375°F (190°C) for 15 to 18 minutes, flipping them halfway through the cooking time. Cook until the chicken reaches an internal temperature of 165°F (74°C) and the exterior turns a beautiful golden brown.
7. Once the chicken is cooked through, remove it from the air fryer and let it rest for a minute or two.
8. Transfer the Air Fried Honey Mustard Chicken to serving plates and garnish with fresh parsley for a pop of color and freshness.
9. Serve this delightful dish alongside your favorite side dishes like steamed vegetables or fluffy rice to complete your wonderful meal for two.

35. SZECHUAN GREEN BEANS

Ingredients

- 10 ounces (280g) fresh green beans, trimmed
- 1 tablespoon vegetable oil
- 1 tablespoon soy sauce
- 1 tablespoon rice vinegar
- 1 teaspoon Szechuan peppercorns, crushed
- 1 teaspoon red pepper flakes (adjust to your preferred spice level)
- 2 garlic cloves, minced
- 1 teaspoon fresh ginger, grated
- 1 tablespoon sesame oil
- 1 tablespoon toasted sesame seeds
- 2 green onions, thinly sliced (for garnish)

1. Preparation: Rinse and trim the fresh green beans, ensuring they are all similar in size for even cooking. Crush the Szechuan peppercorns using a mortar and pestle, and mince the garlic cloves. Grate the fresh ginger, and thinly slice the green onions for garnish.
2. Preheat the Air Fryer: Preheat your air fryer to 400°F (200°C) for 5 minutes to ensure it's hot and ready for cooking.
3. Sauce Preparation: In a small bowl, whisk together the vegetable oil, soy sauce, rice vinegar, crushed Szechuan peppercorns, red pepper flakes, minced garlic, and grated ginger until well combined.
4. Toss the Green Beans: Place the trimmed green beans in a mixing bowl and drizzle with the sesame oil. Toss the beans to ensure they are evenly coated with the oil.
5. Coating with Sauce: Pour the prepared sauce over the green beans and toss until they are fully coated, allowing the flavors to infuse the beans.
6. Air Frying: Arrange the sauced green beans in a single layer in the air fryer basket, ensuring they have enough space for proper air circulation. Cook in the preheated air fryer at 400°F (200°C) for 8-10 minutes, or until the beans are tender and slightly crispy.
7. Topping: Once cooked, transfer the air-fried green beans to a serving platter and sprinkle with toasted sesame seeds and thinly sliced green onions for an extra burst of flavor and presentation.
8. Serve and Enjoy: Serve the Szechuan Green Beans as a delectable side dish alongside your favorite Chinese main course. Savor the enticing blend of Szechuan spices, the satisfying crunch of the beans, and the lingering taste of garlic and ginger.

36. FRIED SALT AND PEPPER PRAWNS

Ingredients

- 10 ounces (283 grams) raw prawns, peeled and deveined
- 1 tablespoon cornstarch
- 1 teaspoon sea salt
- 1 teaspoon freshly ground black pepper
- 1/2 teaspoon garlic powder
- 1/2 teaspoon onion powder
- 1/4 teaspoon cayenne pepper (adjust to taste)
- 1 tablespoon vegetable oil
- Fresh cilantro or parsley leaves for garnish
- Lemon wedges, for serving

1. Preparation: In a large bowl, pat dry the prawns with a paper towel. This ensures the seasoning sticks well to the prawns during cooking.
2. Seasoning Mix: In a separate bowl, combine the cornstarch, sea salt, black pepper, garlic powder, onion powder, and cayenne pepper. Mix the seasoning well to create a uniform blend.
3. Coating the Prawns: Drizzle the vegetable oil over the prawns and toss to coat them evenly. Sprinkle the seasoning mix over the prawns and toss again, ensuring each prawn is coated thoroughly.
4. Preheat the Air Fryer: Preheat your air fryer to 400°F (200°C).
5. Air Frying: Place the seasoned prawns in the air fryer basket in a single layer, leaving some space between them to ensure even cooking. You may need to cook them in batches if your air fryer is small.
6. Air Fry First Side: Air fry the prawns for 5 minutes, then carefully flip them over using tongs.
7. Air Fry Second Side: Continue air frying for an additional 3-4 minutes or until the prawns turn golden and crispy.
8. Serve: Transfer the air-fried salt and pepper prawns to a serving plate. Garnish with fresh cilantro or parsley leaves. Serve hot with lemon wedges on the side for a zesty tang.

37. SESAME TERIYAKI WINGS

Ingredients

- 12 chicken wings
- 2 tablespoons sesame oil
- 2 tablespoons soy sauce
- 2 tablespoons honey
- 1 tablespoon rice vinegar
- 1 tablespoon mirin
- 2 cloves of garlic, minced
- 1 teaspoon grated ginger
- 1 tablespoon sesame seeds
- 2 green onions, finely sliced

1. Preheat your air fryer to 400°F (200°C). This ensures your wings will emerge perfectly crispy and golden in no time.
2. In a bowl, combine the sesame oil, soy sauce, honey, rice vinegar, mirin, minced garlic, and grated ginger. Stir the mixture well, creating a tantalizingly sweet and savory teriyaki marinade.
3. Place the chicken wings into a large resealable plastic bag and pour the teriyaki marinade over them. Seal the bag, then give it a gentle shake, ensuring the wings are fully coated in the delectable sauce. Allow the flavors to meld for about 30 minutes.
4. Remove the wings from the marinade and place them in a single layer inside your preheated air fryer. You want them to be well-spaced to encourage even cooking and achieve that crispy texture we all adore.
5. Cook the wings in the air fryer for 18-20 minutes, flipping them over halfway through the cooking time to ensure they're cooked evenly. The wings should emerge beautifully golden and crispy, ready to delight your senses.
6. While the wings are cooking, gently toast the sesame seeds in a dry pan over low heat until they become lightly golden and aromatic.
7. Once the wings are done, transfer them to a serving dish and sprinkle the toasted sesame seeds on top, allowing their nutty essence to enhance the dish.
8. Garnish the wings with finely sliced green onions, adding a vibrant touch to the presentation.

38. SESAME TERIYAKI CAULIFLOWER

Ingredients

- 1 small head of cauliflower, cut into bite-sized florets
- 2 tablespoons soy sauce
- 1 tablespoon hoisin sauce
- 1 tablespoon rice vinegar
- 1 tablespoon sesame oil
- 1 tablespoon honey
- 1 tablespoon grated fresh ginger
- 2 garlic cloves, minced
- 1 tablespoon cornstarch
- 1 tablespoon water
- 1 tablespoon vegetable oil
- 1 tablespoon sesame seeds
- 2 green onions, thinly sliced (for garnish)

1. Preheat your air fryer to 375°F (190°C).
2. In a bowl, whisk together soy sauce, hoisin sauce, rice vinegar, sesame oil, honey, grated ginger, and minced garlic to make the ginger garlic sauce.
3. In a separate small bowl, mix the cornstarch with water until fully dissolved to create a slurry.
4. Place the cauliflower florets in a large mixing bowl and pour half of the ginger garlic sauce over them. Toss to coat the cauliflower evenly.
5. Transfer the coated cauliflower to the air fryer basket, shaking off any excess sauce, and drizzle 1 tablespoon of vegetable oil over the cauliflower.
6. Air fry the cauliflower at 375°F (190°C) for 15 minutes, shaking the basket halfway through for even cooking.
7. After 15 minutes, open the air fryer and drizzle the cornstarch slurry over the cauliflower, tossing gently to combine.
8. Sprinkle sesame seeds over the cauliflower and air fry for an additional 3-4 minutes until the cauliflower is tender and the coating is slightly crispy.
9. Remove the air fryer basket and transfer the Sesame Teriyaki Cauliflower to a serving plate.
10. Garnish with sliced green onions and serve immediately alongside steamed jasmine rice or noodles for a complete and satisfying meal for two.

39. CRISPY SWEET AND SPICY AIR FRIED CALAMARI

Ingredients

- 8 ounces (225g) fresh calamari, cleaned and sliced into rings
- 1/4 cup (60ml) honey
- 2 tablespoons (30ml) soy sauce
- 1 tablespoon (15ml) Sriracha sauce (adjust according to your spice preference)
- 1 teaspoon (5ml) sesame oil
- 1/2 teaspoon (2.5ml) garlic powder
- 1/4 teaspoon (1.25ml) ground ginger
- 1/4 cup (30g) all-purpose flour
- 1/4 cup (30g) cornstarch
- Cooking spray or oil mister

1. Preheat your air fryer to 400°F (200°C).
2. In a bowl, combine honey, soy sauce, Sriracha sauce, sesame oil, garlic powder, and ground ginger. Stir well to create the sweet and spicy glaze.
3. In a separate bowl, mix all-purpose flour and cornstarch until combined.
4. Dip the calamari rings into the flour mixture, shaking off any excess.
5. Generously coat the air fryer basket with cooking spray or use an oil mister to lightly spray the basket.
6. Place the coated calamari rings in a single layer in the air fryer basket, making sure they don't touch each other.
7. Air fry the calamari at 400°F (200°C) for 8-10 minutes, turning them halfway through the cooking time to ensure even crispiness.
8. Once the calamari rings turn golden and crispy, remove them from the air fryer and place them in a clean bowl.
9. Pour the sweet and spicy glaze over the cooked calamari, tossing gently to coat each ring evenly.

40. FRIED HONEY SOY GLAZED TOFU

Ingredients

- 8 ounces (226g) firm tofu, drained and pressed
- 2 tablespoons soy sauce
- 1 tablespoon honey
- 1 tablespoon sesame oil
- 1 teaspoon grated ginger
- 1 teaspoon minced garlic
- 1 tablespoon cornstarch
- 1 tablespoon water
- 1 tablespoon sesame seeds, for garnish
- 1 green onion, sliced, for garnish

1. Preheat Air Fryer: Preheat your air fryer to 375°F (190°C) for 5 minutes.
2. Prepare Tofu: Cut the tofu into bite-sized cubes. Blot them gently with paper towels to remove any excess moisture.
3. Create Glaze: In a small bowl, mix together soy sauce, honey, sesame oil, grated ginger, and minced garlic. Set the glaze aside.
4. Coat Tofu: In a separate bowl, combine cornstarch and water to create a slurry. Dip each tofu cube into the slurry, ensuring they are evenly coated.
5. Air Fry Tofu: Place the coated tofu cubes in the preheated air fryer basket in a single layer, leaving space between each cube. Air fry at 375°F (190°C) for 12-15 minutes or until the tofu turns golden and crispy. Remember to shake the basket halfway through to ensure even cooking.
6. Glaze Tofu: Once the tofu is done, transfer it to a large mixing bowl. Pour the honey soy glaze over the tofu and gently toss until all the pieces are coated with the glaze.
7. Garnish and Serve: Sprinkle sesame seeds and sliced green onions over the glazed tofu for an extra burst of flavor and a touch of elegance. Serve the Air Fried Honey Soy Glazed Tofu alongside steamed jasmine rice or your favorite stir-fried vegetables.

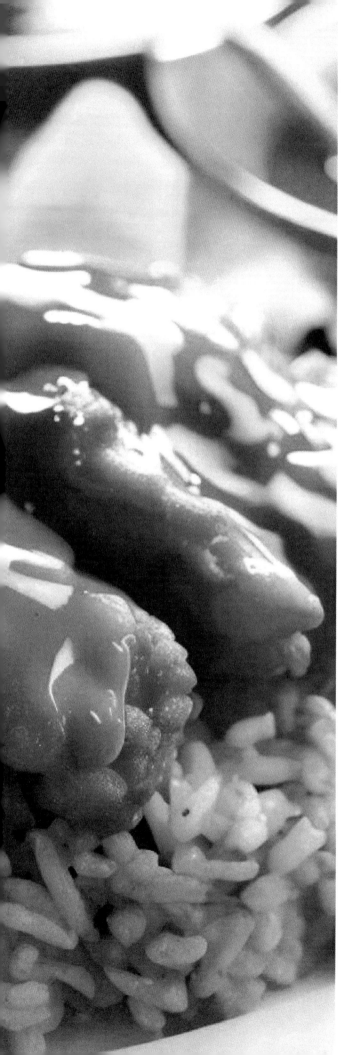

41. CANTONESE-STYLE AIR FRIED CHICKEN

Ingredients

- 2 boneless, skinless chicken breasts, cut into bite-sized pieces
- 2 tablespoons soy sauce
- 1 tablespoon oyster sauce
- 1 tablespoon hoisin sauce
- 1 tablespoon Shaoxing wine (Chinese rice wine) (substitute: dry sherry)
- 1 tablespoon honey
- 1 teaspoon sesame oil
- 2 garlic cloves, minced
- 1-inch piece of fresh ginger, grated
- 2 tablespoons cornstarch
- 2 tablespoons all-purpose flour
- 1/4 teaspoon salt
- 1/4 teaspoon black pepper
- Cooking spray or oil mister

1. In a medium-sized bowl, whisk together the soy sauce, oyster sauce, hoisin sauce, Shaoxing wine, honey, sesame oil, minced garlic, and grated ginger. This aromatic marinade will infuse the chicken with enticing flavors. (Temperature: Preheat air fryer to 370°F (188°C)).
2. Place the bite-sized chicken pieces into the marinade, ensuring each piece is well coated. Cover the bowl with plastic wrap and let it marinate in the refrigerator for at least 30 minutes, allowing the flavors to meld and the chicken to tenderize.
3. In a separate bowl, combine the cornstarch, all-purpose flour, salt, and black pepper. This will be the coating for the marinated chicken, giving it a delightful crunch.
4. Take the marinated chicken from the refrigerator and drain off any excess marinade. Dredge each piece of chicken in the flour mixture, pressing gently to ensure an even coating.
5. Prepare your air fryer basket by lightly spraying it with cooking spray or using an oil mister to coat the surface. This will prevent the chicken from sticking and promote a beautiful golden color.
6. Place the coated chicken pieces in the air fryer basket in a single layer, making sure they don't touch each other. Cook in batches if needed, maintaining the correct spacing.
7. Air fry the chicken at 370°F (188°C) for 8-10 minutes, flipping the pieces halfway through the cooking time. The chicken should be golden and crispy on the outside and fully cooked through on the inside.
8. Once done, transfer the air-fried Cantonese-style chicken to a serving plate. Garnish with chopped scallions or sesame seeds for an extra touch of elegance and a hint of nutty flavor.

42. HONEY GARLIC SHRIMP

Ingredients

- 12 large shrimp, peeled and deveined
- 2 tablespoons honey
- 2 tablespoons soy sauce
- 2 cloves garlic, minced
- 1 tablespoon olive oil
- 1/2 teaspoon grated fresh ginger
- 1/2 teaspoon sesame oil
- 1/4 teaspoon red pepper flakes (optional)
- Freshly ground black pepper, to taste
- Chopped green onions, for garnish
- Sesame seeds, for garnish
- Lime wedges, for serving

1. Preheat the air fryer to 400°F (200°C).
2. In a mixing bowl, combine the honey, soy sauce, minced garlic, olive oil, grated ginger, sesame oil, and red pepper flakes (if using). Whisk the ingredients together until well blended to create the flavorful marinade.
3. Add the peeled and deveined shrimp to the bowl of marinade. Toss the shrimp gently to coat each one thoroughly with the luscious mixture. Let them sit and marinate for about 10 minutes, allowing the flavors to infuse.
4. Arrange the marinated shrimp in a single layer in the air fryer basket. Sprinkle freshly ground black pepper over the shrimp for an extra burst of flavor.
5. Slide the basket into the preheated air fryer and cook the shrimp for 5-6 minutes, flipping them halfway through the cooking time. The shrimp should be beautifully golden and crispy on the outside.
6. Once done, transfer the succulent shrimp to a serving plate, garnishing with chopped green onions and sesame seeds for an irresistible visual and textural appeal.
7. Accompany the Air Fried Honey Garlic Shrimp with lime wedges on the side, providing a zesty finish that complements the sweetness of the dish.

43. MONGOLIAN TOFU

Ingredients

- 14 oz (400g) firm tofu, cubed into bite-sized pieces
- 2 tablespoons cornstarch
- 2 tablespoons vegetable oil
- 2 cloves of garlic, minced
- 1/2 teaspoon grated fresh ginger
- 3 tablespoons soy sauce
- 2 tablespoons hoisin sauce
- 1 tablespoon brown sugar
- 1/4 cup water
- 1 teaspoon sesame oil
- 1/4 teaspoon red pepper flakes (optional)
- 2 green onions, sliced (for garnish)
- Toasted sesame seeds (for garnish)

1. Preheat your air fryer to 400°F (200°C).
2. Gently pat dry the tofu cubes using paper towels to remove any excess moisture.
3. Place the cornstarch in a shallow bowl and toss the tofu cubes in it until evenly coated.
4. Brush the air fryer basket with 1 tablespoon of vegetable oil to prevent sticking. Arrange the cornstarch-coated tofu cubes in a single layer in the air fryer basket.
5. Air fry the tofu for 10 minutes until it turns crispy and golden. Pause halfway to shake the basket gently to ensure even cooking.
6. Meanwhile, in a small saucepan over medium heat, add the remaining 1 tablespoon of vegetable oil and sauté the minced garlic and grated ginger until fragrant.
7. Lower the heat and add the soy sauce, hoisin sauce, brown sugar, water, sesame oil, and red pepper flakes (if using). Stir well and let the sauce simmer for a couple of minutes until it thickens slightly.
8. Once the tofu is done, transfer the crispy tofu cubes to a mixing bowl.
9. Pour the prepared Mongolian sauce over the tofu and gently toss until the tofu is coated evenly.
10. Return the sauced tofu to the air fryer basket and air fry for an additional 5 minutes to allow the flavors to meld together.
11. Carefully remove the air fryer basket and serve the delectable Mongolian tofu on a serving dish. Garnish with sliced green onions and toasted sesame seeds for an enticing finishing touch.
12. Serve hot alongside steamed jasmine rice or your favorite stir-fried vegetables. Savor the tender, caramelized goodness of Mongolian Tofu, an exquisite masterpiece created right in your very own kitchen.

44. SPICY GREEN BEANS WITH GROUND PORK

Ingredients

- 8 oz (225g) fresh green beans, washed and trimmed
- 6 oz (170g) ground pork
- 2 tablespoons vegetable oil
- 1 tablespoon soy sauce
- 1 tablespoon oyster sauce
- 1 tablespoon chili garlic sauce (adjust to your preferred spice level)
- 1 tablespoon rice vinegar
- 1 teaspoon sesame oil
- 2 cloves garlic, minced
- 1/2-inch (1.25cm) fresh ginger, grated
- 2 green onions, sliced (white and green parts separated)
- Sesame seeds, for garnish
- Cooked white rice, for serving

1. Preheat your air fryer to 400°F (200°C).
2. In a small bowl, combine soy sauce, oyster sauce, chili garlic sauce, rice vinegar, and sesame oil. Mix well to create the spicy sauce.
3. Place the fresh green beans in a mixing bowl and drizzle with 1 tablespoon of vegetable oil. Toss until the beans are evenly coated with oil.
4. Transfer the green beans to the air fryer basket, spreading them out in a single layer.
5. Cook the green beans in the air fryer for 5 minutes, shaking the basket halfway through to ensure even cooking.
6. While the green beans cook, heat the remaining 1 tablespoon of vegetable oil in a skillet over medium-high heat. Add minced garlic, grated ginger, and the white parts of the green onions. Sauté for 1-2 minutes until fragrant.
7. Add the ground pork to the skillet and cook until it's no longer pink, breaking it into small crumbles as it cooks.
8. Pour the spicy sauce mixture over the cooked ground pork and stir to combine. Reduce the heat to low and let it simmer for 2-3 minutes until the sauce thickens slightly.
9. Once the green beans are done in the air fryer, add them to the skillet with the ground pork and sauce. Toss everything together until the green beans are evenly coated with the spicy sauce.
10. Transfer the spicy green beans and ground pork to a serving dish.
11. Garnish with the green parts of the sliced green onions and a sprinkle of sesame seeds.

45. SALT AND PEPPER OKRA

Ingredients

- 8 ounces (225g) fresh okra, washed and trimmed
- 1 tablespoon olive oil
- 1/2 teaspoon sea salt
- 1/2 teaspoon freshly ground black pepper
- 1/4 teaspoon garlic powder
- 1/4 teaspoon onion powder
- 1/4 teaspoon chili powder (adjust to your desired level of spiciness)
- Fresh cilantro leaves, for garnish (optional)

1. Prepare the Okra: Wash the fresh okra thoroughly under cold running water and trim off the stem ends. Pat them dry with a kitchen towel or paper towel.
2. Preheat the Air Fryer: Preheat your air fryer to 400°F (200°C) for about 5 minutes. This will ensure even cooking and a beautiful crispy texture.
3. Season the Okra: In a large mixing bowl, drizzle the okra with olive oil, coating each piece evenly. Then, sprinkle the sea salt, freshly ground black pepper, garlic powder, onion powder, and chili powder over the okra. Give it a gentle toss to coat the okra with all those delightful flavors.
4. Air Frying Delight: Place the seasoned okra in the preheated air fryer basket in a single layer. Make sure they have a little space between them for the hot air to circulate. Cook the okra in the air fryer at 400°F (200°C) for 10-12 minutes, or until they turn golden brown and become wonderfully crispy.
5. Serve and Savor: Once the okra is done, transfer them to a serving plate, and if desired, garnish with fresh cilantro leaves for an added touch of brightness. Serve immediately as a scrumptious side dish or a delectable appetizer.

46. LEMON GINGER SALMON

Ingredients

- 2 salmon fillets (6 oz each)
- 2 tablespoons fresh lemon juice
- 2 teaspoons grated fresh ginger
- 1 tablespoon olive oil
- 1 teaspoon honey
- 1 teaspoon soy sauce
- 1/2 teaspoon garlic powder
- 1/2 teaspoon salt
- 1/4 teaspoon black pepper
- Lemon wedges, for serving
- Fresh parsley, chopped, for garnish

1. Preheat the air fryer to 390°F (199°C) for 5 minutes.
2. In a small bowl, whisk together the fresh lemon juice, grated ginger, olive oil, honey, soy sauce, garlic powder, salt, and black pepper until well combined.
3. Place the salmon fillets in a shallow dish and pour the lemon ginger marinade over them, making sure they are evenly coated. Let them marinate for about 15 minutes to allow the flavors to infuse.
4. Carefully remove the salmon fillets from the marinade and transfer them to the air fryer basket, skin side down. Reserve the marinade for later use.
5. Place the basket in the preheated air fryer and cook the salmon at 390°F (199°C) for 8-10 minutes, depending on the thickness of the fillets. The salmon should be opaque and easily flake with a fork when it's done.
6. While the salmon is cooking, pour the reserved marinade into a small saucepan. Bring it to a gentle simmer over medium heat, stirring occasionally, until it thickens slightly into a luscious glaze.
7. Once the salmon is done, carefully remove it from the air fryer and place it on a serving plate.
8. Drizzle the warm lemon ginger glaze over the salmon fillets, allowing it to cascade down the sides enticingly.
9. Garnish with chopped fresh parsley and serve the Lemon Ginger Salmon alongside lemon wedges for an extra citrusy punch.

47. SWEET AND SOUR TOFU

Ingredients

- 14 oz (400g) firm tofu, drained and cubed
- 1/4 cup (60ml) pineapple juice
- 2 tablespoons ketchup
- 1 tablespoon rice vinegar
- 1 tablespoon soy sauce
- 1 tablespoon brown sugar
- 1 teaspoon grated ginger
- 1 teaspoon cornstarch
- 1 tablespoon vegetable oil
- 1/2 small red bell pepper, diced
- 1/2 small green bell pepper, diced
- 1/2 small onion, diced
- 1/4 cup (60ml) vegetable broth
- 1/4 cup (60ml) water
- 1 tablespoon chopped green onions (scallions), for garnish
- Cooked white rice, to serve

1. Preheat your air fryer to 400°F (200°C).
2. In a bowl, whisk together pineapple juice, ketchup, rice vinegar, soy sauce, brown sugar, grated ginger, and cornstarch to make the sweet and sour sauce. Set aside.
3. Place the cubed tofu in a separate bowl and toss gently with 1 tablespoon of vegetable oil, ensuring each piece is coated evenly.
4. Carefully place the tofu cubes in a single layer in the air fryer basket. Cook for 10 minutes, shaking the basket halfway through for even browning.
5. In the meantime, heat a tablespoon of vegetable oil in a pan over medium heat. Add the diced red and green bell peppers, and onion. Sauté until slightly softened, about 2-3 minutes.
6. Pour the sweet and sour sauce over the sautéed vegetables and stir well. Add vegetable broth and water, stirring continuously until the sauce thickens slightly. Simmer for another 2 minutes.
7. Once the tofu is done in the air fryer, add it to the sweet and sour sauce in the pan. Gently toss to coat the tofu with the sauce.
8. Serve the Air Fried Sweet and Sour Tofu over a bed of cooked white rice. Garnish with chopped green onions for added freshness and flavor.

48. FRIED KUNG PAO CAULIFLOWER

Ingredients

- 1 medium-sized cauliflower head, cut into bite-sized florets
- 2 tablespoons vegetable oil
- 1/4 cup unsalted peanuts or cashews
- 3-4 dried red chili peppers, deseeded and cut into small pieces
- 2 cloves garlic, minced
- 1-inch piece of ginger, finely grated
- 1 green onion, sliced (both white and green parts)
- 2 tablespoons soy sauce
- 1 tablespoon hoisin sauce
- 1 tablespoon rice vinegar
- 1 tablespoon honey
- 1/2 teaspoon Szechuan peppercorns, crushed (optional, for an extra spicy kick)

1. Preheat your air fryer to 375°F (190°C) while you prepare the ingredients.
2. In a large mixing bowl, toss the cauliflower florets with 1 tablespoon of vegetable oil until evenly coated.
3. Place the cauliflower florets in the preheated air fryer basket, ensuring they are in a single layer. Cook for 15 minutes, shaking the basket halfway through the cooking time to ensure even cooking.
4. While the cauliflower is air frying, heat the remaining 1 tablespoon of vegetable oil in a skillet or pan over medium heat.
5. Add the peanuts or cashews to the skillet and toast them until they turn lightly golden. Remove them from the skillet and set them aside.
6. In the same skillet, add the dried red chili peppers, minced garlic, and grated ginger. Sauté for a minute or until fragrant, being careful not to burn the garlic.
7. Lower the heat and add the sliced green onions (keep some for garnish) to the skillet, reserving the remaining green parts for garnish.
8. Stir in the soy sauce, hoisin sauce, rice vinegar, honey, and crushed Szechuan peppercorns (if using) into the skillet. Mix well and let the sauce simmer for 2-3 minutes until it thickens slightly.
9. Once the cauliflower is done air frying, transfer it to a large mixing bowl and pour the Kung Pao sauce over it. Toss gently until the cauliflower is evenly coated with the sauce.

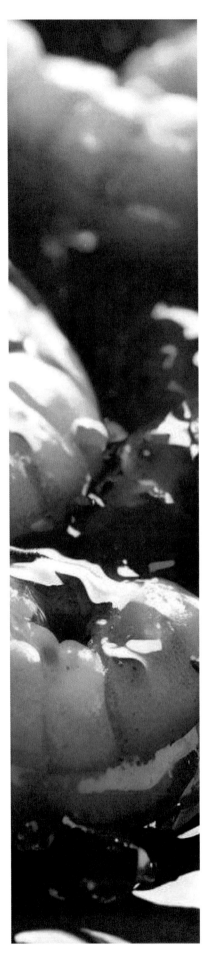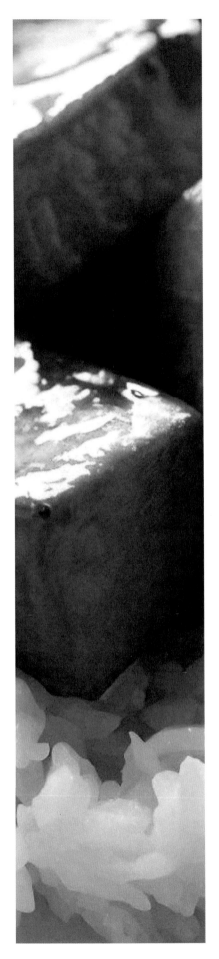

49. GARLIC
BUTTER SHRIMP

Ingredients

- 1/2 lb (225g) large shrimp, peeled and deveined
- 2 tablespoons unsalted butter, melted
- 2 cloves garlic, minced
- 1 tablespoon fresh lemon juice
- 1 tablespoon chopped fresh parsley
- 1/4 teaspoon salt
- 1/4 teaspoon black pepper
- Pinch of red pepper flakes (optional)

1. Preheat the Air Fryer: Preheat your air fryer to 400°F (200°C) for about 5 minutes, allowing it to reach the optimum cooking temperature.
2. Prepare the Garlic Butter Sauce: In a microwave-safe bowl, melt the butter. Add the minced garlic, lemon juice, chopped parsley, salt, black pepper, and a pinch of red pepper flakes if you desire a hint of heat. Stir the mixture until well combined.
3. Coat the Shrimp: Place the peeled and deveined shrimp in a separate bowl. Pour the prepared garlic butter sauce over the shrimp and toss until they are evenly coated.
4. Arrange the Shrimp in the Air Fryer Basket: Arrange the coated shrimp in a single layer in the air fryer basket, ensuring they have some space between each other for even cooking.
5. Air Fry the Shrimp: Slide the basket into the preheated air fryer and cook the shrimp at 400°F (200°C) for 8-10 minutes. Turn the shrimp halfway through the cooking time to ensure they cook evenly.
6. Check for Doneness: After the cooking time is up, check that the shrimp are opaque and cooked through.
7. Serve and Enjoy: Once the shrimp are perfectly cooked, transfer them to a serving plate and drizzle any remaining garlic butter sauce over the top. Garnish with a sprig of fresh parsley, and they are ready to be served! This garlic butter shrimp pairs wonderfully with steamed rice or a fresh garden salad.

50. HONEY BBQ WINGS

Ingredients

- 1 lb (450g) chicken wings, tips removed and separated into drumettes and flats
- 2 tablespoons honey
- 2 tablespoons BBQ sauce
- 1 tablespoon vegetable oil
- 1 teaspoon smoked paprika
- 1/2 teaspoon garlic powder
- 1/2 teaspoon onion powder
- 1/2 teaspoon salt
- 1/4 teaspoon freshly ground black pepper
- Fresh cilantro or parsley, for garnish (optional)

1. Preheat the Air Fryer: Preheat your air fryer to 380°F (193°C) for about 5 minutes to ensure it's nice and hot before we start cooking our delectable wings.
2. Prepare the Wings: In a large mixing bowl, toss the chicken wings with vegetable oil, smoked paprika, garlic powder, onion powder, salt, and black pepper. Ensure the wings are well coated with the flavorful seasoning.
3. Air Fry the Wings - First Round: Place the seasoned wings in the preheated air fryer basket in a single layer, making sure they have some space around each piece for optimal crispiness. Air fry the wings at 380°F (193°C) for 10 minutes, flipping them halfway through the cooking process to ensure even browning.
4. Prepare the Glaze: While the first round of air frying is underway, mix the honey and BBQ sauce in a small bowl until well combined, creating the luscious glaze for our wings.
5. Coat the Wings: After the initial 10 minutes, remove the partially cooked wings from the air fryer and generously brush them with the honey BBQ glaze, coating each piece thoroughly.
6. Air Fry the Wings - Second Round: Return the glazed wings to the air fryer basket and continue air frying at 380°F (193°C) for another 5-6 minutes, or until the wings turn gorgeously golden and irresistibly crisp.
7. Garnish and Serve: Once fully cooked and gloriously glazed, take the wings out of the air fryer and let them rest for a minute or two. Optionally, garnish with some fresh cilantro or parsley for a burst of vibrant flavor.

In this, my latest culinary endeavor, I invite you on a tantalizing journey through the rich tapestry of Chinese cuisine, reinvented for the modern kitchen with the ingenious touch of an air fryer. With an artful blend of traditional flavors and contemporary cooking techniques, this recipe book promises to be your passport to creating authentic Chinese dishes with ease and flair. Through its pages, you'll discover 50 delectable recipes, from succulent Honey Sesame Chicken and crispy Salt and Pepper Squid to aromatic Mongolian Beef, all made effortlessly and healthily using the magic of the air fryer.

I've strived to demystify the intricate world of Chinese cooking, infusing it with my signature ease and passion for flavors. From savory dim sum delights to sweet and spicy sensations, each recipe is meticulously crafted to awaken your taste buds and evoke the vibrant essence of Chinese cuisine. Whether you're a seasoned chef or an enthusiastic home cook, this book promises to be your trusted companion, guiding you through the steps of creating authentic Chinese dishes that are both impressive and satisfying.

Embark on this culinary voyage and let my collection of wonderful recipes become your kitchen companion, empowering you to unlock the secrets of time-honored Chinese flavors with the modern convenience of the air fryer. With every turn of the page, you'll embrace the joy of cooking, revel in the sizzling aromas, and savor the tastes of China right in the comfort of your own home.

All my love,
Julia Narvey

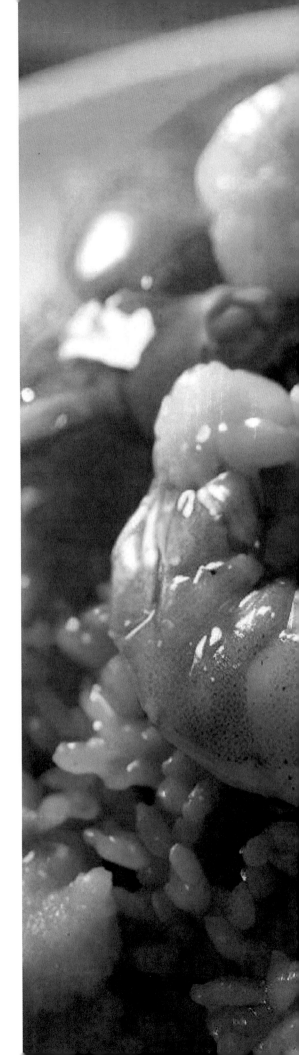